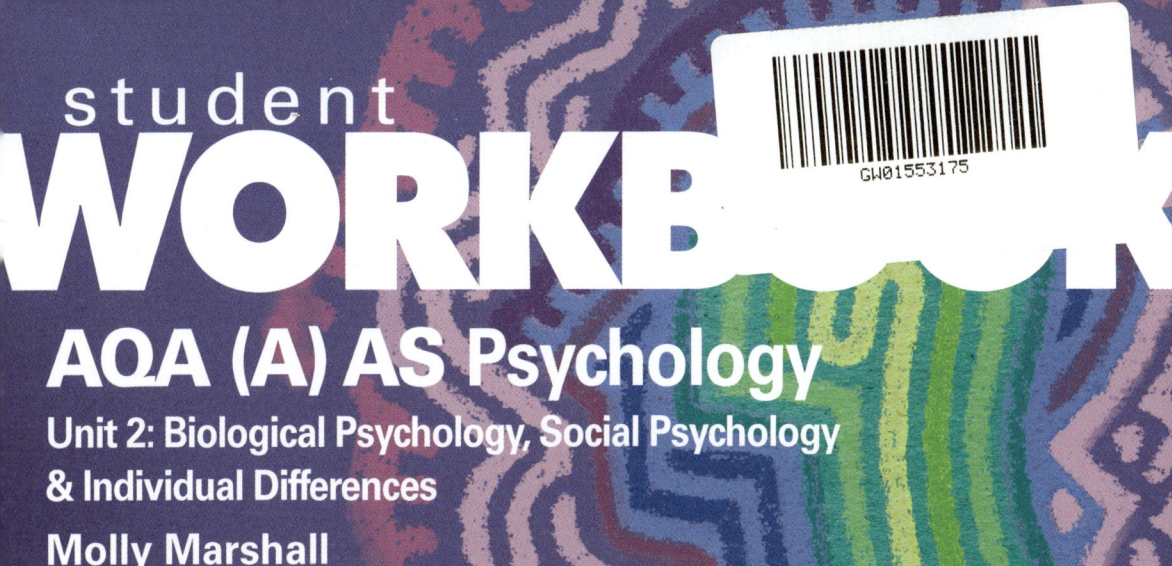

Introduction		2
Section 1	**Biological psychology**	
Topic 1	Stress as a bodily response	3
Topic 2	Stress in everyday life	16
Section 2	**Social psychology**	
Topic 1	Social influence	37
Topic 2	Social influence in everyday life	52
Section 3	**Individual differences**	
Topic 1	Psychological abnormality	59
Topic 2	Treating psychological abnormality	74

Philip Allan Updates, an imprint of Hodder Education, part of Hachette Livre UK, Market Place, Deddington, Oxfordshire OX15 0SE

Orders
Bookpoint Ltd, 130 Milton Park, Abingdon, Oxfordshire OX14 4SB

tel: 01235 827720, fax: 01235 400454

e-mail: uk.orders@bookpoint.co.uk

Lines are open 9.00 a.m.–5.00 p.m., Monday to Saturday, with a 24-hour message answering service. You can also order through the Philip Allan Updates website: www.philipallan.co.uk

© Philip Allan Updates 2008

ISBN 978-0-340-96681-5

First printed 2008

Impression number 5 4 3 2 1

Year 2013 2012 2011 2010 2009 2008

All rights reserved; no part of this publication may be reproduced, stored in a retrieval system, or transmitted, in any form or by any means, electronic, mechanical, photocopying, recording or otherwise without either the prior written permission of Philip Allan Updates or a licence permitting restricted copying in the United Kingdom issued by the Copyright Licensing Agency Ltd, Saffron House, 6–10 Kirby Street, London EC1N 8TS.

Printed in Spain

Hachette Livre UK's policy is to use papers that are natural, renewable and recyclable products and made from wood grown in sustainable forests. The logging and manufacturing processes are expected to conform to the environmental regulations of the country of origin.

Introduction

The aim of this workbook is to help you increase your understanding of biological psychology, social psychology and the psychology of individual differences, and to improve your skills in answering the types of question you might encounter in the AQA (A) AS examination.

It presents a variety of stimulus material that will help you to learn about psychological research, terminology and concepts. The questions are designed to support you as you develop skills of analysis, interpretation and evaluation. They are progressively more difficult within each topic. Writing answers will help you learn to communicate your knowledge and understanding of psychology in a clear and effective manner. As you complete the workbook, you should become confident that you are learning the content required for the exam and how to write effective answers that will achieve high marks.

The workbook follows the AQA (A) specification. It is organised into three sections.

Section 1 Biological psychology

Topic 1 focuses on the body's response to stressors, including the general adaptation syndrome (Selye) and research into the relationship between stress and physical illness, including the effects of stress on the immune system. Topic 2 looks at the sources of stress, including life changes and workplace stressors. This topic also focuses on methods of managing the negative effects of stress, including physiological treatments and psychological approaches.

Section 2 Social psychology

Topic 1 looks at research studies into conformity and explanations of why people yield to majority influence (conformity) and minority influence. Topic 2 focuses on explanations of the psychological processes involved in conformity and obedience, and the reasons why people obey and how people might resist obedience.

Section 3 Individual differences

Topic 1 deals with attempts to define and explain psychological abnormality and their limitations and at key features of biological and psychological models of abnormality. Topic 2 focuses on treating abnormality and includes biological and psychological therapies.

You can study either Section 1, Section 2 or Section 3 of this workbook first. To gain maximum benefit, you should complete the topics and questions in the order given within each section. There are several ways in which you can use this workbook:
(1) As an integral part of your learning experience, in conjunction with your class notes, handouts and textbook.
(2) As a revision tool, in which case you should work through the topics, writing the answers as practice for the exam.
(3) As a combination of **(1)** and **(2)**: if, as you progress through the module, you write answers to all the questions in this book, at the end of the course you will have created a valuable resource from which to revise!

Whichever way you choose, I hope the workbook will help you in your studies and in your exam.

Section 1 Biological psychology

Topic 1 Stress as a bodily response

I expect you know what it feels like to be stressed. Perhaps you have experienced stress before an exam, when your heart beats faster and your palms start to sweat. In this topic, you will learn how psychologists explain the physiology (the bodily responses) of stress. Physiological psychology focuses on biological explanations of behaviour, such as how and why the brain and nervous system respond to stressors.

Item 1
What is stress?

Stress is a type of alarm reaction, involving heightened mental and bodily states. It is both a psychological and a physiological response to the environment. Your brain produces a stress reaction when you are in a situation that is physically or mentally demanding. **Stress is normal** and some stress is good for you — it keeps you alert and protects you in times of danger or when you need to act or think quickly. Physical fitness training places stress on your body, but that stress has a beneficial effect. Feeling a bit stressed about exams is normal — it may help you to focus your energy on revising well. However, prolonged and unwanted stress may lead to mental and physical health problems.

When psychologists talk about 'stress', they may refer to the **causes** of stress reactions (stressors) or to the **effects** of stress reactions on our physical and mental functioning. Stress can be explained as a stimulus in the environment that causes a stress response. For example, if you worry about exams, a forthcoming exam could be defined as a 'stressor', and your rapid heart rate and sweating palms before the exam could be explained as the 'stress response'.

Of course, not everyone worries about exams. Thus, stress can be defined as the response that happens when **we think we cannot cope** with a stressor in the environment. If we think we cannot cope, we feel stress and when we feel stress, we experience physiological changes.

Item 2
The hypothalamic–pituitary–adrenal axis

The stress response originates in the hypothalamus and includes the pituitary and adrenal glands. This hypothalamic–pituitary–adrenal axis is responsible for arousing the autonomic nervous system (ANS) in response to a stressor.

Under stress, the sympathetic branch of the nervous system stimulates the adrenal gland to release adrenaline, noradrenaline and corticosteroids into the bloodstream. This produces the physiological reactions, such as increased heart rate and blood pressure and a dry mouth, known as the 'fight or flight' response.

Item 3
The general adaptation syndrome (GAS)

Selye (1956) proposed that stress leads to a depletion of the body's resources, leaving the animal vulnerable to illness. He used the word 'stress' to describe the fact that many different stimuli (fear, pain, injury) all produce the same response. He called these 'stressors' and proposed that the body reacts in the same general way to all these stressors by producing a response which helps the animal adapt to the stressors and continue to function. Selye called this the 'general adaptation syndrome' (GAS) and identified three stages in the model.

1. **Alarm** When we perceive a stressor, the ANS responds. Adrenaline, noradrenaline and corticosteroids (hormones) are released into the bloodstream. The bodily reaction is increased arousal levels in readiness for a physical response (fight or flight), i.e. the heart rate increases, blood pressure rises and muscles tense.
2. **Resistance** If the stressor continues, the bodily reaction (the fight or flight response) ceases and we appear to be coping, but output from the adrenal cortex continues and the adrenal glands may become enlarged.
3. **Exhaustion** If the stressor continues for a long time, the body is unable to cope. The body's resources are reduced but alarm signs, such as increased blood pressure, may return. The person may become depressed and unable to concentrate. The immune system may be damaged and stress-related diseases, such as stomach ulcers, high blood pressure and depression, are more likely to occur.

Item 4
Mary and Jim have a stressful day

It was a fine sunny day and Mary was pushing her new baby in his buggy in the park. As she rounded the corner by the paddling pool, a huge dog rushed towards her, growling and barking. She was terrified of dogs and in a panic she started to run.

Jim woke up with a sinking feeling in his chest. He had failed to win the new client and his manager was not going to be pleased. As he dressed, he switched on the radio and heard there was a 20-mile traffic jam on the M25. Now he would be late again. He hated his job, and had done for months. He threw his clothes on and, hearing the telephone ring, swore and ran downstairs.

Stress-related illness
Item 5
Stress and cardiovascular disorders

Cardiovascular disorders are disorders of the heart and blood vessels and are sometimes linked with stress. People who experience stress may engage in unhealthy activities, such as smoking

Topic 1 Stress as a bodily response

and drinking alcohol in an attempt to relieve the stress. These behaviours increase the likelihood that the person will develop a cardiovascular disorder, so stress may cause illness indirectly.

Long-term stress may also have a direct effect on the cardiovascular system. Stress causes high heart rate and high blood pressure. Long-term stress can damage blood vessels, because adrenaline and noradrenaline contribute to increases in blood cholesterol levels, leading to blood clots and thickened arteries. Weakened or damaged blood vessels may cause haemorrhages, which in turn may lead to blockages in blood vessels, causing strokes or heart attacks.

Item 6
Research into the effect of stress on blood flow (Krantz et al. 1991)

In this study, the direct effect of stress on blood flow and blood pressure was investigated. Thirty-nine participants performed a stress-inducing task (e.g. a maths test) while their blood pressure and rate of blood flow to the heart was measured. The stressful task caused a reduced blood flow to the heart and led to raised blood pressure. From this it was concluded that stress has a direct effect on the cardiovascular system, making cardiovascular disorders more likely.

Item 7
Friedman and Rosenman (1974)

Cardiologists Friedman and Rosenman defined two types of behaviour pattern, Type A and Type B:
- **Type A behaviour.** Type A people move, walk, eat and talk rapidly, and try to do two or more things at one time. In personality, Type A people are competitive and tend to judge themselves by the number of successes they have, rather than the quality of their successes. Type A individuals are hard-driving, impatient and aggressive. They tend to be achievement-orientated and hostile. In physiology, Type A people have a higher level of cholesterol and fat in their bloodstream, have a more difficult time getting the cholesterol out of their bloodstream, and have a greater likelihood of clotting within the arteries.
- **Type B behaviour.** Type B people seldom feel any sense of time urgency or impatience, are not preoccupied with their achievements or accomplishments and seldom become angry or irritable. They tend to enjoy their recreation, are free of guilt about relaxing, and they work calmly and smoothly.

Aims Based on their observations of patients who displayed the common Type A behaviour pattern of impatience, competitiveness and hostility, Friedman and Rosenman aimed to test their belief that Type A personalities were more prone to coronary heart disease (CHD) than Type B personalities.

Procedures The sample comprised 3000 male volunteers, all from California, USA, aged between 39 and 59, who were healthy at the start of the study. Personality type was established through the use of a structured interview and observations of the participants' behaviour during the interview. The interviewer interrupted the interview from time to time to deliberately annoy Type A individuals. The answers to questions and behavioural responses were used to assess participants' impatience, competitiveness and hostility.

Findings Eight and a half years later, 257 of the men in the sample were diagnosed as having CHD. Seventy percent of those with CHD had been classified as Type A. The Type A men were also found to have higher levels of adrenaline and cholesterol. Twice as many Type A men had died as compared with Type Bs. Type As also had higher blood pressure, higher cholesterol and other symptoms of CHD. Type As were more likely to smoke and have a family history of CHD, both of which would increase their risk.

Conclusion Type A personality is associated with illness and symptoms of CHD. Because Type A is also linked to other factors that cause CHD, such as smoking, it is not certain whether Type A is a direct or an indirect cause of CHD.

Criticisms
- This was a long-term study with a large sample having a baseline measure (all the men were free of CHD at the start of the study).
- The study showed how psychological factors (personality) are related to physiological factors (CHD).
- The study cannot show that Type A personality causes CHD. It may be that Type A behaviours develop as a result of long-term stress.
- Categorising all men into two personality types is reductionist. Later research has identified Type C and D personalities.
- The sample was both gender biased and ethnocentric (all males from the USA) and as such cannot be generalised to females.

The findings of **Williams (2000)** support Friedman and Rosenman in their description of Type A personalities as hostile. In the Williams study, 13 000 participants completed questionnaires asking about their feelings of anger, and the participants' responses were rated for anger scores. Six years later, those with high anger scores were significantly more likely to have suffered a heart attack.

Item 8
Stress and the immune system

The immune system comprises billions of cells that travel through the bloodstream. They are produced in the bone marrow, spleen, lymph nodes and thymus. The major type of immune cells is white blood cells, which defend the body against antigens — bacteria, viruses and cancerous cells. Some types of immune cells produce antibodies that destroy antigens.

When we are stressed, the ability of the immune system to protect us against antigens is reduced, leading to an increased likelihood of physical illness. This weakening of the immune system is called the '**immunosuppressive effect of stress**'. In long-term stress, such as stage 3 of Selye's GAS, increased levels of corticosteroids can reduce the production of antibodies (a direct effect).

Topic 1 Stress as a bodily response

Item 9
Kiecolt-Glaser et al. (1984): stress and the immune system

Based on the assumption that the body's response to stress reduces the effectiveness of the immune system (immunosuppression), Kiecolt-Glaser et al. aimed to establish a link between stress and reduced immune system functioning.

Aims To look for evidence of a difference in immune response in high- and low-stress conditions, and to see whether factors such as anxiety were associated with immune system functioning.

Procedures Seventy-five first-year medical students (49 male and 26 female) volunteered to give blood samples 1 month before their final exams, and after they had sat two papers on the first day of the exams. The blood samples were analysed for how much 'natural killer cell' activity was present (natural killer cells help to protect against viruses). The students also completed questionnaires to assess symptoms of depression and loneliness, and to find out what other stressful events they might be experiencing.

Findings In comparison with the first blood sample, natural killer cell activity was significantly reduced in the second sample. It was most reduced in those students who were experiencing other stressful events, and in those who reported feeling anxious and depressed.

Conclusion Stress has an immunosuppressant effect and can be associated with reduced immune system function.

Criticisms
- The study has high mundane realism as the exams were real-life experiences and would have happened anyway.
- The first blood sample acted as a baseline control and the participants were being compared against themselves — this controlled for the effects of personality variables.
- It is not possible to say that no other variable could have caused the change in the students' immune systems as other variables could not be controlled (e.g. it might have been lack of sleep due to long hours revising that affected the immune system).
- It is not possible to say how long-lasting the reduced effectiveness of the immune system might be

Item 10
Kiecolt-Glaser et al. (1995): the effect of stress on wound healing

The immune system is involved in helping the body repair itself after injury. Following tissue damage (cuts and wounds), the immune system produces interleukin B, which promotes healing by helping to create scar tissue.

Aim To show that stress has an indirect effect on wound healing, due to reduced effectiveness of the immune system.

Procedures The study involved 13 women who cared for relatives suffering from Alzheimer's disease (the high-stress group), and a control group of 13 women who had no stressful responsibilities (the no-stress group). All the women gave skin samples which caused skin wounds.

Findings The wounds of the carers in the high-stress group took, on average, 9 days longer than those of the no-stress group to heal. It was concluded that long-term stress reduces the effectiveness of the immune system to heal wounds.

Criticisms
- The study is useful to NHS staff, as it may explain why the wounds of some patients take longer to heal than expected.
- The sample was small and all female, and it may not be safe to generalise the findings to other populations.
- There was no baseline measure of how rapidly the wounds might have healed in the high-stress group before the onset of the stressor.

Item 11
Can you help Dr Jamadi?

Dr Jamadi is baffled. Pansy and Dahlia are two of his elderly patients. He has been treating them for ulcers on their legs. Ulcers are difficult to treat and he has been very careful. Over the past 2 weeks, both women, whose ulcers are similar, have received the same treatment. In the case of Pansy, the ulcers are responding to treatment and are improving. In the case of Dahlia, the ulcer shows little sign of improvement. He is worried about Dahlia who, following her recent bereavement, seems to be depressed and anxious.

Questions

1 Read your textbook and Item 1. Complete the following sentences.

   a A stressor is

   b Stress can be defined as

Topic 1 Stress as a bodily response

....

....

2 Read your textbook and Item 2. Use the words in the list below to fill in the blanks in this description of the hypothalamic–pituitary–adrenal axis.
- dilated
- mouth
- pituitary
- hypothalamus
- physiological
- gland
- bloodstream
- adrenal
- adrenaline

The stress response originates in the .... and includes the .... and .... glands. This hypothalamic–pituitary–adrenal axis is responsible for arousing the autonomic nervous system (ANS) in response to a stressor. When under stress, the sympathetic branch of the nervous system stimulates the adrenal .... to release ...., noradrenaline and corticosteroids into the .... This produces the .... reactions, such as increased heart rate and blood pressure, ... pupils and dry ...., known as the 'fight or flight' response.

3 Read Item 2. Reorder these sentences so that they represent the correct sequence of the hypothalamic–pituitary–adrenal axis.

.... The ANS is activated.

.... The pituitary gland releases adrenocorticotrophic hormone into the bloodstream.

.... A signal is sent to the hypothalamus.

.... This stimulates the adrenal cortex to release corticosteroids.

.... This stimulates the adrenal medulla to release adrenaline and noradrenaline.

.... A message is sent to the pituitary gland.

.... The evaluation of a stressor occurs in the cerebral cortex.

.... This leads to an increase in heart rate and blood pressure.

4 Read your textbook and Item 3.

Complete the right-hand column of the table to produce a model of Selye's GAS.

	Description of Selye's GAS
Stage 1	
Stage 2	
Stage 3	
Reasons for link between stress and illness	
Strength(s)	
Weakness(es)	
Conclusion	

5 Read Item 4.

a Referring to Selye's GAS, explain which stage of the syndrome Mary may be in, the physiology of what is happening to Mary and why it is happening.

Topic 1 Stress as a bodily response

b Explain which stage of the syndrome Jim may be in, and the possible threats to his health.

6 Read your textbook and Items 1, 2 and 3. Selye's GAS can be described as a 'reductionist' model. Explain why.

7 Read your textbook and Items 5 and 6.

  a Explain what is meant by 'cardiovascular disorders'.

  b Outline *one* way in which stress may be an indirect cause of cardiovascular disorders.

  c Outline *one* way in which stress may be a direct cause of cardiovascular disorders.

8 Read your textbook and Item 7. Write a synopsis of the aims, procedures, findings and conclusions of the research described in Item 7.

Aims

Procedures

Findings

Conclusions

9 Read your textbook and Item 7. List *two* criticisms of research that conclude that stress may be related to cardiovascular disorders.

10 Read your textbook and Item 8.

　a Outline what is meant by the 'immune system'.

Topic 1 Stress as a bodily response

b Explain how stress may reduce the effectiveness of the immune system.

c What does 'stress is an immunosuppressant' mean?

11 Read your textbook and Item 9. Outline the aims, procedures, findings and conclusions of the study of the relationship between stress and the immune system described in Item 9.

Aims

Procedures

Findings

Conclusions

12 Read Items 9 and 10. Outline *two* criticisms of research into the relationship between stress and the immune system.

13 Read your textbook and Items 9, 10 and 11. From what you know about Pansy and Dahlia, and from what you have learned about research into the relationship between stress and the immune system, write a letter to Dr Jamadi (quoting research evidence) to explain why Dahlia's ulcer may take longer to heal than Pansy's.

Topic 1 Stress as a bodily response

14 *Exam practice*

Review the items on stress and physical illness. To what extent has psychological research demonstrated a link between stress and reduced effectiveness of the immune system?

Write a list of points as an outline plan for this essay. In your outline, identify the evaluative points you will discuss and the evidence you will use to justify your arguments.

Try to use one of these phrases for each evaluation point you list:
- One strength of this research is…
- On the other hand…
- This implies that…
- This is useful because…
- Not all psychologists agree, for example…

These findings are reliable/unreliable because

Topic 2 Stress in everyday life

Life seems to be stressful much of the time, and there are many sources of stress — traffic jams, long queues at the supermarket, crying babies, too many exams (you could make your own list). Perhaps the two major sources of stress are work and changes in an individual's life.

- **Life events.** Throughout our lives we experience many changes, such as leaving home, going to university, getting married, changing employment, the birth of children and moving house. These events cause us to change the way we live, and adjusting to change may cause stress.
- **The workplace.** Going to work can be stressful. For some people, the kind of work they do, where they work and with whom they work can be a source of stress. Some of the more stressful occupations are nursing, teaching, social work and the emergency services. Someone who is stressed at work may become ill and need to take time off. Employers are concerned about stress at work, because productivity is reduced when employees suffer from stress-related illness.

Understanding stress would be easy if we all responded to similar stressors in the same way. But, of course, we do not. Some people seem to thrive on lifestyles that others would find very stressful. In this topic, you will learn about the sources of stress and what psychologists know about individual differences in responding to stressors.

Life changes and daily hassles

Item 1
Holmes and Rahe (1967): social readjustment rating scale (SRRS)

Aims (i) To construct an instrument for measuring stress (stress was defined as the amount of life changes people had experienced during a fixed period).

(ii) To show that the amount of life changes (i.e. the amount of stress) is related to psychological and physiological illness.

Procedures The medical records of 5000 patients were examined and a list was compiled of the 43 life events that appeared in the 12 months before their illnesses. One hundred people (the 'judges') were told that the life event of marriage had been rated at 50 points. They were then asked to rate how much readjustment each of the 43 life events would require 'relative to marriage'.

Findings (i) Death of a spouse was thought to require twice as much adjustment as marriage and was rated at 100 points by the judges. The average for each of the 43 life events was calculated. Holmes and Rahe could now rank the 43 life events from death of a spouse (at 100 points) to minor violations of the law (11 points). A questionnaire was designed in which participants ticked the life events they had experienced in the last 12 months, thus giving a measure of the amount of life change (stress) they had experienced.

Topic 2 Stress in everyday life

(ii) People with high scores on the SRRS (over the previous 12 months) were likely to experience some physical illness. A person having 300 points over 12 months had an 80% chance of becoming ill, and illnesses ranged from heart attacks to diabetes and sports injuries.

Conclusions (i) Stress can be objectively measured by the SRRS as a life changes score.
(ii) High scores on the SRRS (high-stress scores) predict physical illness, and stressful life changes cause physical illness.

Criticisms
- The research provides an objective measure of the relationship between stress and illness. Supporting evidence was found from a study in which 2500 navy personnel completed the SRRS before they left for a 6-month trip on board their ships. Health records were kept which found that high scores on the SRRS correlated with physical illness.
- The experience of a life event is different for each person — for example, some people may be distressed by divorce whereas others are relieved. Life events other than the 43 on the SRRS may also cause stress, for example having your home flooded. In addition, most of the 43 life events are infrequent and the daily small hassles of life may be a more significant cause of stress.

DeLongis et al. (1982)

DeLongis et al. (1982) theorised that everyday hassles caused stress. They created a hassles scale to assess the effect of the routine problems of life, such as getting stuck in a traffic jam. The hassles scale measures positive events (uplifts) as well as hassles. In people over 45, they found that the hassles scale was a better predictor of ill health than life changes (SRRS). The frequency and intensity of hassles correlated significantly to ill health.

Workplace stress
Item 2
The six areas of stress in the workplace

1. **Interpersonal factors.** Relationships with bosses, colleagues and customers may be stressful. Social support is very important in moderating the effects of stress in general. Good relationships with co-workers can reduce stress in the workplace; poor relationships at work can exacerbate stress.
2. **Work pressure.** Having too much work to do and working to strict deadlines can cause stress.
3. **The physical environment.** This may be noisy, hot and overcrowded, or may involve health risks and unsociable hours, such as working night shifts. **Czeisler et al. (1982)** researched the causes of health problems and sleep difficulties experienced by employees of a chemical plant in Utah, USA. The employees worked shifts. He recommended that the pattern of shifts should be changed to a 21-day shift rotation and always 'shift forward' (phase advance). After 9 months, job satisfaction and productivity increased.
4. **Role stress.** Worry about job security or responsibility may cause stress.

5 **Role conflict.** Having to express one emotion while feeling another may cause stress, e.g. doctors, nurses, police.
6 **Control.** How much control people have over how they do a job may be a factor in how stressful the job is perceived to be.

> ### Johnson and Hall (1988): the importance of control and interpersonal relationships at work
>
> **Aim** To investigate the relationship between variables in the workplace (social support, perceived control and how demanding jobs are) and the incidence of cardiovascular disease.
>
> **Procedures** Data from 14000 male and female Swedish workers were analysed to explore the relationship between cardiovascular disease and job stress, specifically stress associated with control, demand and social support. The data included four scales of measurement:
> 1 Work control, based on questions about the level of influence over the planning of work.
> 2 Work-related social support, based on questions about how and when workers could interact with co-workers.
> 3 Psychological demands of work, based on questions about how demanding the work was.
> 4 An indicator of cardiovascular health.
>
> **Findings**
> - Jobs that were perceived to be demanding but which involved low levels of control were related to increased incidences of heart disease.
> - Where workers had fewer social interaction opportunities (low social support), there was an increase in cardiovascular disease in the high demand, high control combination.
> - Low social support combined with low control increased cardiovascular disease.
>
> **Conclusion** Both social support and control are important factors in work-related stress.
>
> **Criticisms**
> - This research shows how factors such as control and social support at work are important in understanding workplace stress.
> - Self-reports may result in inaccurate descriptions of job characteristics and may be biased by personality characteristics.
> - Workplaces are complex. Using objective measures of workplace stress may result in a reductionist approach that overemphasises the social context of stress. Qualitative research is required in order to understand the meaning of events for individuals.

Factors that may cause stress in the workplace

Role conflict in the workplace

Margolis and Kroes (1974) found that when the demands of the organisation conflict with the needs of the workers, stress may result. They found that when the job requires workers to express one emotion, e.g. being calm and cheerful, while really feeling another emotion, e.g. being unhappy or worried, this causes role conflict. Nurses, teachers and paramedics are likely to suffer stress caused by role conflict.

Topic 2 Stress in everyday life

Is having control at work important?

Marmot et al. (1997) investigated whether perceived control is an important factor in work-related stress. In their study, 7000 civil service employees who worked in London participated in a survey. Data were gathered on how senior they were (their employment grade) and how much control and support they perceived they had at work. Five years later, the medical histories of the employees were reviewed. The participants who were less senior (lower grades) and who felt they had less control and less social support were more likely to have cardiovascular disorders. It was concluded that how much control people have at work, and how much social support people receive from colleagues, may be factors in whether they suffer from stress-related illness.

Item 3
Nelson's stressful life

Nelson is a gunner with a tank crew. He has just been promoted to sergeant. This led to his family being relocated to Germany, so they moved house. They moved twice last year. They used to be a happy family, but now Nelson's teenage daughter hates her new school and blames him because she has no friends. His wife is miserable in Germany and she dislikes their new house. Nelson is due to leave for a 6-month tour of duty in Iraq and is anxious about leaving his family. He and his wife row all the time, he feels guilty and he cannot sleep at night. On top of all his worries, Nelson has started to make mistakes. Yesterday, he missed his practice target three times and the tank commander bawled him out in front of the whole crew. Still, he and his mates had a good laugh about that afterwards.

Individual differences in response to stressors

Item 4
Personality differences and stress

The **Type A personality**, especially the hostile Type A personality, is significantly associated with coronary heart disease. The **Type C personality**, hardworking, conventional and sociable, responds to stress with a sense of helplessness and may be more likely to suffer from cancer. In support of this, **Morris et al. (1981)** found a link between people who tended to suppress their anger and the increased incidence of cancer.

Helgeson and Fritz (1999) studied nearly 300 patients receiving treatment for blocked arteries. Six months later, they found that those patients who were lowest in 'cognitive adaptation' were three times more likely to have experienced a new coronary event. High cognitive adaptation included an ability to develop a positive outlook about one's medical condition and a sense of control in most situations. They concluded that the 'pessimist personality' is more likely to become ill as a result of stress.

Kobasa (1979) proposed that some people are better able to deal with stress (the hardy personality) and that all people could learn to behave in this way in order to cope better. The key traits of a hardy personality, known as the three Cs, are having a strong sense of personal *control*, a strong sense of purpose (*commitment*) and the ability to see problems positively, as *challenges* to be overcome rather than as stressors.

Gender differences and stress

More men suffer from coronary heart disease than women, and there are several explanations as to why gender may be an important factor in stress:
- women are biologically more able to cope with stress
- women are socialised to cope better with stress
- women tend to drink and smoke less and may do less stressful work

From an **evolutionary (biological) perspective**, men should respond to situations of danger with the 'fight or flight' arousal response, whereas women should respond by looking after young ones and each other. **Taylor et al. (2000)** reviewed many biological and behavioural studies (both human and animal) and concluded that females were more likely to deal with stress by nurturing those around them and reaching out to others. Men were more likely to hide away or start a confrontation. This suggests different responses to stress that match gender types.

From a **social perspective**, males and females are socialised in different ways. Women learn to use social networks more and this may reduce their stress. Women are taught to think about social conflict situations differently. **Vögele et al. (1997)** proposed that females learn to control their anger and react more calmly in stressful situations, but males learn that anger is an acceptable response and feel stress if they have to suppress anger. **Iso et al. (2002)** looked at 73 000 Japanese participants aged 40–79. Participants were asked to rate the level of stress in their daily lives. Over the following 8 years, those Japanese women who reported high levels of mental stress were more than twice as likely to die from stroke and heart disease than women reporting low stress levels.

There may also be **gender differences in lifestyles**. Women engage in fewer unhealthy behaviours than men, e.g. they smoke and drink less. Perhaps the Western stereotype that 'men do not talk about their feelings' leads men to resort to drinking and smoking as a way of coping with stress.

Item 5
Stress management

There are many ways of coping with stress, and the effectiveness of the coping strategy depends on the type of stressor and the characteristics of the person who is trying to cope.

Stress management refers to therapies used by doctors in clinical situations and to coping strategies taught by psychologists. It can also refer to the informal ways in which people try to cope with stress in their lives. Psychologists categorise coping strategies as:
- physiological or psychological
- emotion-focused or problem-focused

Topic 2 Stress in everyday life

Physiological approaches to stress management help people cope by changing the way the body responds to stress. They focus on the reduction of physical symptoms of stress.

Psychological approaches to stress management help people cope by getting them to think about their problems in a different way. Such approaches focus on encouraging people to deal with the causes of their stress. One psychological approach is to increase the sense of control people have in stressful situations.

Emotion-focused approaches may attempt to reduce the symptoms of anxiety by taking a physiological approach — for example, biofeedback or anti-anxiety drugs may be used.

Problem-focused approaches attempt to change how people respond to stressors, e.g. by using cognitive therapies or by encouraging people to increase their social support.

It is important to note that emotion-focused and problem-focused approaches are not exclusive categories, as problem-focused approaches also deal with emotions.

Item 6
Physiological approaches to stress management

Drugs

Drugs aim to reduce the physiological, or bodily, response to stress. Two drugs which do this are benzodiazepine and beta-blockers.

Benzodiazepine is an anti-anxiety drug and its brand names include Librium and Valium. These drugs slow the activity of the central nervous system (CNS) and reduce anxiety by enhancing the activity of a natural biochemical substance, gamma-amino-butyric-acid (GABA). GABA is the body's natural form of anxiety relief and it also reduces **serotonin** activity. Serotonin is a neurotransmitter and people with anxiety need to reduce their levels of serotonin.

Beta-blockers act on the sympathetic nervous system (SNS) rather than the brain. They reduce heart rate and blood pressure and thus reduce the harmful effects of stress.

Advantages of drugs
- They are quick and effective and reduce the physiological effects of stress.
- Many people prefer drug therapies to psychological therapies because 'taking a pill is easy'.
- They do not require people to change the way they think or behave.
- They can be used in conjunction with psychological methods.

Limitations of drugs
- All drugs have side effects. Benzodiazepines can cause drowsiness and may affect memory.
- Long-term use of drugs can lead to physical and psychological dependency.
- They treat the symptoms of stress. Most stresses are psychological and drugs do not address the causes of the problem.

Biofeedback

Biofeedback works because our minds can influence the automatic functions of our bodies. Using a special machine, people can learn to control processes such as heart rate and blood pressure. Biofeedback machines provide information about the systems in the body that are affected by stress. The **electromyogram (EMG)** measures muscle tension. Electrodes are placed on your skin and when tension is detected, the machine gives you a signal. As you become aware of this internal process, you can learn techniques to control tension. Galvanic skin response (GSR) training devices measure electrical conductance in the skin. A tiny electrical current is run through your skin and the machine measures changes in sweat gland ducts. The more emotionally aroused (stressed) you are, the more active your sweat glands are, and the greater the electrical conductivity of your skin.

There are four stages in learning biofeedback:
- The person is attached to a machine that monitors changes in heart rate and blood pressure and gives feedback.
- The person learns to control the symptoms of stress by deep breathing and muscle relaxation; this slows down their heart rate, making them feel more relaxed.
- The biofeedback from the machine acts like a reward and encourages the person to repeat the breathing techniques.
- Through practice, the person learns to repeat the breathing techniques in stressful situations.

Advantages of biofeedback
- There are no side effects.
- It reduces symptoms and gives people a sense of control.
- The learned techniques can be generalised to other stressful situations.
- It is more effective if combined with psychological therapies that encourage people to think about the causes of their stress and how their behaviour may contribute to it.

Limitations of biofeedback
- It requires specialist equipment and expert supervision.
- It requires the stressed person to commit time and effort.
- Very anxious people may find learning biofeedback techniques difficult and it may not be effective therapy for children.

Item 7
Psychological approaches to stress management

Cognitive behavioural therapy (CBT): stress inoculation (Meichenbaum 1985)

The aim of this cognitive behavioural therapy is to prepare people to cope with stress in a similar way to an injection preventing a disease. Training people to deal with stress before it becomes a problem involves three stages:

Topic 2 Stress in everyday life

1 **Conceptualisation** — patients identify and express their feelings and fears. They are encouraged to imagine stressful situations and analyse what is stressful about them and how they might deal with them.
2 **Skill acquisition and rehearsal** — patients practise how to relax and how to express their emotions. Specific skills may be taught, such as positive thinking, communication skills and time-management.
3 **Application and follow through** — patients are supported through progressively more threatening real-life situations while applying the newly acquired skills.

Advantages of stress inoculation
- It focuses on the cause of stress and ways of coping with it.
- It is effective for both short- and long-term stressors and can be combined with other treatment methods.
- The increased feelings of 'being in control' and improved communication and time-management skills lead to increased self-confidence and self-efficacy.
- There are no physiological side effects.

Limitations of stress inoculation
- It may only be successful with patients who are already determined to make the time and effort to help themselves.
- The research findings are based on a narrow sample (mainly white middle-class, well-educated people), thus they may not generalise to other populations.

Increasing hardiness (Kobasa 1977)

The aim of increasing hardiness is to encourage people to respond to stressors in a positive manner instead of perceiving them as disasters, and to teach the behavioural, physiological and cognitive skills that enable them to cope with stressors. Hardiness training involves three stages:
1 **Focusing** — patients are taught to recognise the signs of stress, such as muscle tension and tiredness, and to identify the sources of the stress.
2 **Re-living stressful encounters** — patients are asked to re-live stressful situations and to analyse these situations so that they can learn from past experience.
3 **Self-improvement** — patients use the insights gained so that they see stressors as challenges that can be coped with, leading to improved self-confidence and an enhanced sense of personal control.

Advantages of increasing hardiness
- Evidence suggests this approach is effective. Williams et al. (1992) found that 'high' hardy people use more problem-focused and support-seeking measures when dealing with stress than 'low' hardy people, who tend to use avoidance and wishful thinking. Hardiness is associated with successful coping strategies.
- As with stress inoculation, hardiness training focuses on coping with the causes of stress.
- It can be combined with other treatment methods and improves self-confidence and self-efficacy.

Limitations of increasing hardiness
- The research findings are based on an all-male sample and may not generalise to females.
- It may only be successful with patients who see stress as a challenge to be coped with.
- The concept of hardiness is complex, and in very stressful situations even hardy personalities may succumb to anxiety and negative thinking.

Item 8
The role of control in stress management

Psychological research suggests that the role of control in managing stress is important. Having a sense of 'being in control' has been shown to reduce stress. Psychological approaches to stress management emphasise taking cognitive control, by thinking positively in order to minimise the effects of stressors.

Locus of control (Rotter 1966)

Rotter categorised people into two types. Those having an **external locus of control** believe that good things happen because of luck, and bad things happen because someone else causes them to. People having an external locus of control perceive they have no control and are likely to become anxious in stressful situations. Those having an **internal locus of control** see themselves as responsible for what happens to them and are more likely to take action to manage stressful situations.

The illusion of control (Glass and Singer 1972)

In this study, two groups of participants were exposed to loud noise. In the experimental condition, participants were deceived into believing they could control the noise by pressing a button. In the control condition, participants were simply exposed to loud noise. Galvanic skin response (GSR) was used to measure the stress response (arousal levels) of both groups. The experimental group who believed they had control showed lower arousal levels (reduced stress response). It was concluded that people who believe they are in control in stressful situations, even if they actually have no control, are less likely to become stressed.

Langer and Rodin (1976)

In a controlled study, residents in an old people's home were given more personal control over their lives. Those who had choices and who were able to make decisions were more active, happier and lived longer. Those who had no control were less active and less healthy.

Item 9
Hypothetical case studies

Ranjit is 38. For 2 years he has been working on a large project that involves monthly travel between the UK, France and Spain and he is tired and stressed. He has been to his doctor, who has told him that his blood pressure is significantly raised and that he is suffering from chronic stress.

Topic 2 Stress in everyday life

Robert is 49. He works shifts and has just moved into a new flat. The students who live next door play loud music at all hours of the day and night. Robert feels anxious and stressed. Some days when the music starts he wonders how he can carry on. He doesn't feel he can take control of the situation by confronting the students and wonders whether his doctor can help.

Questions

1 Read your textbook and Item 1. Explain what psychologists mean when they write about 'life change events' and give *two* examples.

....

....

....

....

2 Read your textbook and Item 1.

   a In your own words, explain the difference between a 'life change event' and a 'hassle'.

   ....

   ....

   ....

   b Explain what psychologists mean by an 'uplift'.

   ....

   ....

   ....

   ....

   c Describe the aims, procedures, findings, conclusions and *two* criticisms of *one* study of the relationship between life events and stress.

   Aims

   ....

   ....

   ....

Procedures

Findings

Conclusions

Criticism 1

Criticism 2

d Describe the findings and conclusions of *one* study of the relationship between daily hassles and stress.

Topic 2 Stress in everyday life

3 Outline evidence that suggests that stress can be explained in terms of life changes and list *two* criticisms of this evidence.

Evidence

Criticism 1

Criticism 2

4 Read your textbook and Item 2.

a What is meant by a 'workplace stressor'?

b Item 2 describes several sources of stress in the workplace. Referring to these, outline *one* source of stress you would expect to be present in each of the jobs described here.

Checkout operator in large supermarket

Cleaner in a large comprehensive school

Doctor in a busy town surgery

Staff nurse working nights in an accident and emergency department

Project manager on a North Sea oil-drilling platform

5 Read Item 2. Much research into stress in the workplace involves interviewing people and asking them to complete questionnaires. Suggest one advantage and one disadvantage of using self-report methods to gather data on workplace stressors.

6 Read your textbook and Item 2. Describe the aims, procedures, findings, conclusions and *two* criticisms of *one* study of workplace stressors.

Aims

Procedures

Topic 2 Stress in everyday life

Findings

Conclusions

Criticism 1

Criticism 2

7 Read Item 2. You have just been appointed as manager of human resources in a factory that employs 500 people. The factory makes widgets and production is ongoing, 24 hours a day, 7 days a week. The factory has high levels of sickness and absenteeism. Based on the Johnson and Hall (1988) findings, describe *two* changes to factory procedures that you think may reduce these levels.

8 Review your notes and study Item 3.

  a Make a list of all the stressors in Nelson's life. Based on what you know about Nelson, explain whether Holmes and Rahe would predict that he is likely to suffer a stress-related illness.

  b Suggest whether DeLongis et al. would agree with Holmes and Rahe about Nelson. Give reasons for your suggestions.

9 Read through Item 4.

  a Suggest what psychologists mean by 'individual differences in stress responses'.

Topic 2 Stress in everyday life

b List *two* factors that modify stress.

c Describe *two* effects of personality on stress.

10 Read your textbook and Items 5 and 6.

  a What is the meaning of the term 'stress management'?

  b Outline what is meant by 'physiological approaches to stress management'.

  c Outline what is meant by 'psychological approaches to stress management'.

d Outline what is meant by 'biofeedback'.

e Explain how biofeedback can be used in the physiological approach to stress management. (**Hint:** be clear *why* biofeedback is a physiological approach.)

f Outline *one* advantage and *one* limitation of biofeedback as a method of stress management.

g Explain *two* advantages of using drugs to manage stress. (**Hint:** don't forget to say *why* they are advantages, e.g. 'this is an advantage because…')

Topic 2 Stress in everyday life

h Outline *two* limitations of using drug therapy as a method of stress management. (**Hint:** don't forget to say *why* they are a limitation, e.g. 'this may be a problem because…')

11 Read your textbook and Items 5, 6 and 7.

   a Describe *one* psychological approach to stress management.

   b Explain *two* reasons why psychological approaches to stress management may not always be effective.

c Explain *one* major advantage of using psychological approaches to manage stress. (**Hint:** don't forget to explain *why* it is an advantage.)

....

....

....

12 Read your textbook and Items 5, 6, 7 and 8.

   a Explain what psychologists mean by 'control' in relation to stress management.

....

....

   b Outline the conclusions of psychological research into the role of control in relation to stress.

....

....

....

....

....

....

13 Read Item 9. You are a clinical psychologist and have recently organised a stress-management clinic. Both Ranjit and Robert have been referred for help.

   a Write to Ranjit explaining how chronic stress presents a risk to his physical health and suggesting what action he could take to reduce and manage his high levels of stress.

....

....

....

....

Topic 2 Stress in everyday life

b Write to Robert's doctor outlining recommendations for a stress-management programme for Robert. (**Hint:** Base your recommendations on the research, and outline what you expect the outcomes to be.)

AQA (A) AS Psychology Unit 2 Section 1

14 *Exam practice*

Review your notes and Items 5–8. Evaluate the extent to which psychological approaches to stress management (including the role of control) may be effective in reducing stress.

Write a list of points as an outline plan for this essay. (**Hint:** in your outline, identify the psychological evidence you will use and the evaluative points you will need.)

Try to use one of these phrases for each evaluation point you list:
- One strength of this research is…
- On the other hand…
- This implies that…
- This is useful because…
- Not all psychologists agree, for example…
- There are advantages to X because…

Section 2 Social psychology

Topic 1 Social influence

Social psychology focuses on how we interact with other people and how these interactions may influence our own behaviour. In this topic, you will learn how psychologists have defined social influence and the explanations of why people yield to majority influence (conformity). This topic also looks at psychological explanations of the processes involved in obedience.

Item 1
Definitions

Compliance occurs when a person conforms to the majority opinion but does not agree with it. If group pressure is removed, the conformity will cease. Compliance is thought to occur because an individual wishes to be accepted by the majority group.

Identification occurs when a person conforms to the behaviour expected by the majority, such as obeying school rules about uniform, but without enthusiasm. Identification is thought to occur because an individual wishes to belong to a group.

Informational social influence occurs when a question asked does not have an obviously correct answer. When this happens, people look to others for information and may agree with the majority view. Informational social influence involves the process of compliance.

Internalisation occurs when an individual conforms because he or she believes that a group norm for behaviour or a group attitude is 'right'. If group pressure is removed, this conformity will continue.

Majority influence (conformity) is the process that takes place when an individual's attitudes or behaviour are affected by the views of the dominant group. This may be because of normative social influence (the effect of social norms), but can also occur because of informational social influence, when the minority yields to group pressure because they think that the majority has more knowledge or information.

Minority influence is the process that takes place when a consistent minority changes the attitudes and/or behaviour of an individual. Social psychologists propose that it is the consistency of the minority that is important, since it demonstrates a firm, alternative view to that of the majority. Minority influence leads to a change in attitudes and involves the process of conversion.

Normative social influence occurs when an individual agrees with the opinions of a group of people because he or she wishes to be accepted by them. The influenced individual may not change his or her private belief.

Social influence is the way that a person or a group of people can affect the attitudes and behaviour of another individual.

Item 2
Research studies into conformity

Sherif (1935): conformity as the result of informational social influence

Procedures Participants were shown a still point of light in a dark room. In this situation, an optical illusion called the autokinetic effect occurs when the point of light appears to move. The participants were asked to estimate how far the point of light had moved, first as individuals, then in a group, and finally as individuals again.

Findings In the group estimate condition, participants changed their personal estimate and a group norm emerged. This norm was reflected in their final individual estimates.

Conclusion Since there was no 'factually correct answer', the group norm emerged because individuals looked to others for information.

Asch (1956): conformity as the result of normative social influence

Procedures In a laboratory experiment that used a repeated measures design, groups of seven or eight male students were shown a stimulus line (S) and then three other lines (A, B and C). There was only one 'real' participant in each group. The others were confederates who were helping the experimenter. All the participants were asked to say out loud which line (A, B or C) matched the stimulus line. The real participant always answered last or last but one. Each participant completed 18 trials, and in 12 of the trials (the critical trials), the confederates had all been primed to give the same wrong answer.

Findings In the control trials, the real participants gave incorrect answers 0.7% of the time. In the critical trials, they gave incorrect answers that conformed to the majority view 37% of the time. Of the real participants, 75% conformed at least once. After the experiment, the real participants were asked why they answered as they had. Some said that they did not believe the answers given by the others in the group but they had not wanted to look different.

Conclusion Normative social influence had taken place — the real participants agreed with the opinion of the group because they wished to be accepted by them. This demonstrated that participants gave wrong answers because of compliance rather than conversion.

Item 3
Zimbardo et al. (1973): conformity to social roles

Background There had been a series of violent prison riots in the USA and one explanation for this behaviour was that both prisoners and guards have personalities that make conflict inevitable — prisoners lack respect for authority and guards are attracted to the job because of a desire for power. This is a dispositional hypothesis and

Topic 1 Social influence

it suggests that both prisoners and guards are inevitably 'evil'. Zimbardo suggested that it was possible to separate the effects of the prison environment from the personalities of the inhabitants to test the dispositional hypothesis.

Aims To investigate conformity to social roles and to find out whether conformity is caused by the characteristics of the person (dispositional characteristics), or because of the situation he or she is in (situational factors).

Procedures An advertisement sought male volunteers, to be paid $15 a day, for a study of 'prison life'. The 24 most stable men (physically and mentally) were selected from 75 volunteers. Participants were randomly assigned to the role of either a prisoner or a guard. There were two reserves and one person dropped out, so in the end there were 10 prisoners and 11 guards, all students, and largely middle-class. A mock prison was built in the basement of Stanford University. It had three small cells equipped with a cot for each prisoner, a solitary confinement cell, various rooms for the guards and an interview room. There was also an indoor 'yard' with an observation screen at one end for video-recording equipment and space for observers.

The prisoners remained in prison throughout the study. The guards worked 3-man, 8-hour shifts and were each given a uniform, a whistle, a wooden baton and sunglasses. They were told that they should 'maintain a reasonable degree of order within the prison' but were given no further instructions about how to behave. The prisoners were told to be at home on a particular Sunday. They were 'arrested', booked and fingerprinted and were then blindfolded and driven to the prison. There, they were stripped, deloused and issued with prison uniform: a numbered smock, a light ankle chain, rubber sandals and a cap to make it look like their hair had been shaved off. They were not allowed personal belongings in their cells but were allowed certain 'rights': three meals a day, three supervised toilet trips, 2 hours for reading or letter-writing, and two visiting periods and films per week. They had to line up three times a day to be counted and tested on the prison rules. The guards only referred to the prisoners by number.

Findings The prison environment had a huge impact on the feelings and behaviour of all participants. The guards became sadistic and oppressive. They increased the length of the line-ups until some of them lasted several hours. They decided that the prisoners should only receive their rights as a privilege, in return for good behaviour, and some guards volunteered to do extra hours without pay. Punishments included solitary confinement and humiliation. The prisoners, after short-lived resistance, became passive and depressed. Some coped by becoming sick, whereas others coped by being obedient. Five prisoners had to be released early because of extreme depression (crying, rage and acute anxiety). These symptoms had started to appear within 2 days. The experiment was ended after 6 days, despite the intention to continue for 2 weeks. Even when participants believed they were unobserved, they conformed to their roles.

Conclusions There was strong evidence of conformity to social roles for prisoners and guards. Afterwards, participants reported that they had 'acted out of character', and there was no lasting change in their private opinions. The conformity was due to the social situation rather than to the personal characteristics of the male student participants. Zimbardo suggested that three processes could explain the prisoners' 'submission':
1 **Deindividuation** — the prisoners lost their sense of individuality.
2 **Learned helplessness** — the unpredictable decisions of the guards led the prisoners to give up responding.
3 **Dependency** — the fact that the prisoners depended on the guards for everything emasculated the men and increased their sense of helplessness.

Item 4
Evaluating research into social conformity

Asch (1956)
- **Strengths:** the experimental method leads to meaningful results because there is control over variables. Statements can be made about cause and effect. The study can be replicated.
- **Limitations:** the biased sample of male American students may not be representative of other populations. The study has low mundane validity — it does not represent a lifelike social situation. People may not change their opinions about social variables as readily as they do about line lengths. The study was unethical because Asch deceived the participants.

Zimbardo et al. (1973)
- **Strengths:** this research is useful as it can be applied to improve the situation in real prisons, e.g. by training guards to treat prisoners differently.
- **Limitations:** the artificial situation may have led to demand characteristics. The guards and prisoners may have been acting rather than conforming to their roles. It is possible that media stereotypes of aggressiveness may have influenced the guards' behaviour. Thus the study may not have been a valid measure of conformity to social roles. The prisoners and guards were all young and about the same age. A real prison is an established social community and all the prisoners do not arrive at the same time, so the sample did not represent the population of a real prison.

Item 5
The differences between obedience and conformity

Obedience
- occurs within a social hierarchy
- the emphasis is on social power
- the obedient behaviour is often different from the behaviour of the authority figure
- the motivation for behaviour is explicit
- participants explain their behaviour in terms of obedience

Conformity
- occurs between people of equal status
- the emphasis is on social acceptance
- the conformist behaviour is the same as that of the social group
- the motivation for behaviour is implicit
- participants often deny their behaviour is motivated by conformity

Topic 1 Social influence

Item 6
Milgram (1963): aims and procedures

To obey is to do as one is told to do. Milgram points out that obedience can explain some of the worst examples of human behaviour and that it is a commonly observed social fact that 'the individual who is commanded by a legitimate authority ordinarily obeys'.

Aims Milgram wanted to find out why people obey authority when they are requested to do something unreasonable, what conditions foster obedient behaviour and what conditions foster independent behaviour.

Procedures Milgram advertised, using a newspaper and direct mailing, for men to take part in a study of memory and learning at Yale University. Everyone was paid $4 for coming to the laboratory and they were told that the payment did not depend on remaining in the study for its duration. The chosen participants were 40 men aged between 20 and 50 who came from various occupational backgrounds. There were two further participants: the experimenter was a biology teacher, and the learner (Mr Wallace) was a 47-year-old accountant. Both were confederates of Milgram. The participants were deceived about the purpose of the research. They were told that the aim of the experiment was to see how punishment affected learning. The naïve participant was paired with the confederate and both drew lots to see who would play the part of the 'teacher' and who would be the 'learner'. The confederate always got the part of the learner. The learner was strapped into a chair in the next room attached to an electrode. He was to listen to a list of word pairs and then be given one word and a choice of four possible answers. He was asked to say which of the four was correct. Every time the learner got a question wrong, the teacher would administer an electric shock and the shocks increased in voltage with each mistake. The teacher could see the shock levels displayed on the machine.

The teacher was given a slight shock of 45 volts as a demonstration that the machine was working, but in actuality no other real shocks were given. For the rest of the time, the learner pretended to be receiving shocks. In the experiment, the learner mainly gave wrong answers and for each of these the teacher gave him an electric shock. When the shocks reached 300 volts, the learner pounded on the wall and then gave no response to the next question. When the teacher asked the experimenter for guidance, the experimenter gave the standard instruction, 'an absence of response should be treated as a wrong answer'. After the 315-volt shock, the learner pounded on the wall again but after that, the learner made no other response. If at any time the teacher said he wished to stop, the experimenter used a sequence of four standard 'prods', which were repeated if necessary:

- Prod 1: Please continue.
- Prod 2: The experiment requires that you continue.
- Prod 3: It is absolutely essential that you continue.
- Prod 4: You have no other choice, you must go on.

If the teacher asked whether the learner might suffer permanent physical injury, the experimenter said, 'Although the shocks may be painful, there is no permanent tissue damage, so please go on'. If the teacher said that the learner clearly wanted to stop, the experimenter said, 'Whether the learner likes it or not, you must go on until he has learned all the word pairs correctly. So please go on.'

Item 7
Milgram (1963): findings

The key findings
- Twenty-six of the 40 participants (65%) went all the way to 450 volts with the electric shocks.
- Only nine participants (22.5%) stopped at 315 volts.

Other findings Before the study, Milgram had asked 14 psychology students to predict how participants would behave and the students had estimated that no more than 3% of the participants would continue to 450 volts. People who observed through one-way mirrors were astonished at the participants' behaviour.

The participants showed signs of extreme tension: most of them were observed to 'sweat, tremble, stutter, bite their lips, groan and dig their fingernails into their flesh', and quite a few laughed nervously.

At the end of the study, all the participants were debriefed. They were reunited with the victim, assured there had been no real shocks and told that their behaviour was normal. They were also sent a follow-up questionnaire which showed that 84% felt glad to have participated, and 74% felt they had learned something of personal importance. Only one person reported that he felt sorry to have participated.

Item 8
Milgram (1963): variations on the original experiment and conclusions

The change factors	Percentage of participants who obeyed
Experimenter instructs teacher by telephone (distance order)	23%
Experiment moved from Yale to a scruffy office (less prestige in location)	48%
Teacher in the same room as the learner (increased proximity)	40%
Other teachers refused to give shocks (social support in refusal)	10%
Two teachers, one told by other to give shocks (reduced responsibility)	92.5%
Female participants	65%
Experimenter a member of the public (reduced authority)	20%

Conclusions Milgram concluded that ordinary people will obey orders, in conflict with their conscience, even if this means harming someone else, but that situational factors may determine how people will behave.

Topic 1 Social influence

- **Legitimate authority:** if the person giving the order has legitimate authority, people defer the responsibility for their actions to the authority figure.
- **Agentic state:** people act as agents of the legitimate authority and hold the authority figure responsible for their actions.
- **The slippery slope:** people follow a small 'reasonable' order and then feel obliged to continue when the orders gradually become unreasonable.

Item 9
Milgram (1963): criticisms

Strengths
- The experiment increased the understanding of obedience and the dangers of obedience.
- It made obvious the power relationships between authority figures and those they command.
- Most participants said they were glad they had taken part because they learned something of personal importance.
- The participants believed they were giving shocks (high experimental realism).

Limitations
- There was a lack of informed consent, participants were deceived, and their right to withdraw was breached (though it could be argued that participants could have left), which caused stress.
- The sample was biased as they all were male volunteers.
- The task did not reflect one that would occur in real life — teachers do not give shocks to students who give wrong answers — therefore it had low mundane realism.
- The experiment may have changed the way participants 'saw themselves' and damaged their self-esteem.

Questions

1 Read your textbook and Item 1.

   a Explain what is meant by 'social influence'.

b Complete these sentences.

When a group of people affects the behaviour of another individual, this is an instance of ....

When a person conforms to the majority view in order to be accepted, this is an instance of ....

When a majority changes the attitudes and/or behaviour of the minority, this may be because of ....

When individuals yield to group pressure because they think that the majority has more information, this is an instance of ....

When individuals agree with the opinions of a group of people because they wish to be accepted by them, but they do not change their private belief, this is an instance of ....

c 'The pub was full of Liverpool fans jeering that the Chelsea goal should have been disallowed. "Ain't that right mate," said the chap standing next to Peter. "Too right," Peter replied, though he privately thought the goal had been a fair one.'

In terms of *conformity*, explain why Peter behaved the way he did.

....

....

....

....

d 'Luke told Mai, "General studies is a waste of time, we're all bunking off to the park." Although she enjoyed general studies, Mai agreed to go to the park.'

In terms of *conformity/majority influence*, explain why Mai behaved the way she did.

....

....

Topic 1 Social influence

e Outline *two* explanations for why people may conform to majority influence.

2 Read your textbook and Item 2.

  a Outline the method, sample and procedures used in *one* study of conformity.

AQA (A) AS Psychology Unit 2 Section 2

b In terms of what was being measured, describe the difference between the Asch and the Sherif studies of conformity.

c Evaluate what the Asch study has taught us about the power of normative social influence.

3 Read your textbook and Items 3 and 4.

   a Summarise the findings and conclusions of the Zimbardo prison experiment.

Topic 1 Social influence

b Make *two* suggestions as to how you would reduce anxiety and depression in young prisoners.

c Make *two* suggestions as to how you would reduce the oppressive behaviour of prison guards.

d Based on the limitations of the Zimbardo study, explain why the recommendations you made in **b** and **c** might not be effective.

e Describe *two* ways in which the Asch and Zimbardo studies were similar.

f Suggest *one* change that would increase the validity of the Zimbardo study and explain why this change would be effective.

4 Review Topic 1 and read Item 5 and your textbook.

  a For each of the statements, circle whether the behaviour is best explained by conformity or obedience.

Students at Learnalot School all wear school uniforms	CONFORMITY / OBEDIENCE
People don't park their cars in disabled parking bays	CONFORMITY / OBEDIENCE
Drivers pull over when signalled to do so by the police	CONFORMITY / OBEDIENCE
People wear black clothes at a funeral	CONFORMITY / OBEDIENCE
Soldiers follow the orders of their officers	CONFORMITY / OBEDIENCE

  b Outline *two* differences between conformity and obedience.

Topic 1 Social influence

5 Read Item 6 and study your textbook.

　a Explain the aims of the Milgram research.

　b In Milgram's experiment, explain how the experimenter put verbal pressure on the participants to continue giving electric shocks.

6 Read Items 6, 7, 8 and 9 and your textbook.

　a What percentage of the original 40 participants administered a potentially lethal 450-volt shock?

b Draw a bar chart showing the percentages of obedience levels in the variations of the Milgram study (see item 8).

c Outline *two* reasons why, according to Milgram, people obey authority figures.

d During the experiment, the participants showed signs of suffering stress. Describe the evidence for this and suggest why the participants behaved in this way.

Topic 1 Social influence

e List *two* adaptations to Milgram's experiment that reduced obedience to authority.

f List *two* adaptations to Milgram's experiment that increased obedience to authority.

7 Review Items 6–9. Outline *one* strength and *one* weakness of the Milgram research into obedience to authority.

Topic 2 Social influence in everyday life

This topic looks at explanations of independent behaviour and how people resist pressures to conform or obey. It also examines the influence of individual differences in independent behaviour, and the implications for social change of research into social influence.

Item 1
Factors that affect social conformity

Situational and personal variables will affect the extent to which people conform.

Group size: the bigger the majority, the more influential it will be. In a replication of his original study, Asch tested this and found that with only two confederates, the real participants conformed 13% of the time. With three confederates, the conformity rate rose to 33%, but increasing the number of confederates to more than three had no effect.

Gender: some research suggests that females conform more than males, and that this is because the norm for female behaviour is to be socially orientated (to want to get on with people). However, Eagly and Carli (1981) suggest that experiments which test conformity use tasks that are more familiar to men. The social norms for female behaviour have also changed in the last two decades.

Personality: some people are more self-confident and have higher self-esteem than others. Asch suggested that students conformed less than non-students, and proposed that having a high IQ might be associated with lower levels of conformity.

Culture: people raised in collectivist cultures may be more likely to conform than those raised in individualist cultures, because collectivist cultures value interdependence rather than independence. Smith and Bond (1998) found that Belgian students were less likely to conform (by giving wrong answers) than Indian teachers.

Item 2
Obedience in real-life situations

A case study: Hofling et al. (1966)

Aim To study obedience in a real-life setting.

Procedures Twenty-two nurses working in a hospital were telephoned by an unknown doctor and asked to administer a drug to a patient. The doctor said he would sign the required paperwork later. To obey, the nurses would have to break hospital rules not to take telephone instructions and not to administer drugs unless the paperwork was completed. The dosage instruction was twice the maximum recommended on the drug label.

Topic 2 Social influence in everyday life

Findings Twenty-one nurses obeyed the doctor and would have administered the drug if they had not been stopped. The nurses said that they were often given instructions over the telephone and that doctors were annoyed if they refused.

Conclusion This was a real-life setting in which doctors have high prestige, legitimate authority and power over nurses, and obedience to authority was high.

A case study: Meeus and Raaijmakers (1995)

Aim To study obedience in a real-life setting in Holland.

Procedures At a time of high unemployment in Holland, 24 participants were asked to conduct interviews to test how 'potential job applicants' responded to stress (the job applicants were in fact trained confederates). The participants were prompted to deliver 15 stressful remarks, e.g. 'this job is too difficult for you', designed to cause increasing levels of psychological distress. It was assumed that participants would, when they saw the distress they were causing, refuse to continue. The confederates started out by acting in a confident manner, but then showed distress and eventually begged the interviewer to stop.

Findings In spite of seeing the visible distress they were causing, 22 of the 24 participants delivered all 15 stress-causing remarks.

Conclusion In this realistic face-to-face situation, most participants were obedient and were prepared to cause psychological harm.

Item 3
Obedience and individual differences

Psychologists propose several factors that may be predictors of how likely people are to follow orders.

Personality: Adorno suggested that some people have what is called an 'authoritarian personality', characterised by holding conventional values, being hostile to outgroups, being intolerant to ambiguity and having a submissive attitude to authority. According to Adorno, authoritarian personalities are more likely to obey those in authority.

Moral development: Kohlberg suggested that levels of moral development varied between individuals and that some people reach a level at which their own ethical principles motivate their behaviour. According to Kohlberg, many people operate at a moral level where fear of punishment, or promise of reward, motivates their decisions.

Milgram's findings suggest that people will resist authority when:
- the person giving the order is not present or is 'at a distance', e.g. experimenter instructs teacher by telephone

- the environment in which the order is given does not have high social prestige, e.g. experiment moved from Yale to a scruffy office
- there is peer support for disobedience, e.g. other teachers refused to give shocks
- the person giving the order has no legitimate authority, e.g. experimenter is a member of the public

In summary, people are more likely to **resist obedience** if they:
- are self-confident and able to act independently
- have a high level of moral development
- wish to maintain their autonomy and be 'in control'
- have role models who refuse to obey
- are supported by peers who refuse to obey
- are educated about the dangers of uncritical obedience
- are reminded that they are responsible for the consequences of their actions

Item 5
Obedience today? Woman soldier in abuse spotlight

A female US soldier from West Virginia was identified as apparently abusing Iraqi prisoners. In one of the photographs that shocked the world, Lynndie England is pictured with a leash tied around the neck of a crumpled Iraqi prisoner. In another, she is smiling with a cigarette hanging from her lips, pointing a mock gun at the genitals of a naked prisoner in Baghdad's Abu Ghraib jail. The 21-year-old soldier is being held in detention at Fort Bragg, North Carolina, waiting to hear whether the army will proceed with charges against her. Lynndie England joined the army as a reservist after leaving high school and was sent to Iraq in February 2003, where she found herself helping to guard hundreds of Iraqi prisoners. Five other members of her unit, the 372nd Military Police Company, based in Maryland, are facing proceedings in connection with the alleged abuse. Families and friends of the soldiers have started to speak out. 'They were following orders', a relative of one of the soldiers told the BBC.

Questions

1 Read Item 1. Outline *two* factors that may affect the level of conformity.

Topic 2 Social influence in everyday life

2 a Outline *two* differences between the Milgram study of obedience and the Hofling study of obedience.

b Hofling and Meeus and Raaijmakers were both studies of obedience. Explain whether each of these studies has high or low mundane realism (real-world realism).

c Summarise how research by (a) Milgram, (b) Asch, (c) Zimbardo and (d) Hofling may benefit society by increasing our understanding of social influence.

(Continued overleaf)

AQA (A) AS Psychology Unit 2 Section 2

3 Read your textbook and Item 3.

a Explain why the Adorno theory of 'authoritarian personality' cannot explain the genocide of millions of Jews in concentration camps during the Second World War.

b You have been appointed to advise Notadropincite city council on how to stop people consuming alcohol in the city's parks. Based on psychological research (e.g. Milgram's research findings that demonstrate factors that *maximise* obedience) explain the steps you would take to ensure that this new regulation is obeyed.

Topic 2 Social influence in everyday life

c Regardless of the procedures you have put in place, some people continue to consume alcohol in Notadropincite city's parks. Based on psychological research, give *two* reasons why this disobedience may continue.

4 Read your textbook, all items on social influence in Topics 1 and 2 and Item 5.

a '"They were following orders", a relative of one of the soldiers told the BBC.'

Consider whether psychological research suggests that 'following orders' can adequately explain the shocking behaviour of the soldiers. Write about 150 words.

(**Hint:** You could briefly outline conclusions from research into obedience by Milgram, Hofling, Zimbardo etc., linking these to the soldiers' circumstances and behaviour. You could then evaluate how and where the study procedures are (or are not) similar to the soldiers' circumstances.)

(Continued overleaf)

b Based on evidence from psychological research, outline *two* factors that might increase the soldiers' resistance to following orders.

Section 3 Individual differences

Topic 1 Psychological abnormality

In this topic, you will learn how psychologists define abnormality, including statistical infrequency, deviation from social norms, a failure to function adequately, deviation from ideal mental health and the limitations associated with these definitions. This topic also covers the key features of approaches to psychopathology, including the biological, psychodynamic, behavioural and cognitive approaches.

Item 1
Definitions of psychological abnormality

Abnormality as behaviour which deviates from the statistical norm

Some psychologists propose that behaviour is normally distributed. If this is true, then people whose behaviour is very different — more than two standard deviations (SD) above or below the mean — can be defined as 'abnormal'. The diagram shows that people whose behaviour falls more than three standard deviations above the average will be very rare.

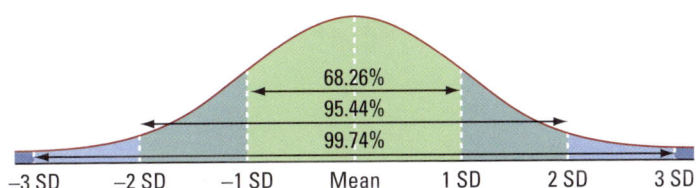

However, this statistical approach has limitations:
- It accounts for the frequency of behaviour, not its desirability. A very low IQ is, statistically, just as abnormal as a very high IQ, but it is desirable to have a high IQ. Therefore, frequency of behaviour tells us nothing about its desirability.
- It does not distinguish between rare behaviour that is eccentric (elective), such as keeping snails as pets, and rare behaviour that is psychologically abnormal, such as schizophrenia.
- It is difficult to define the point at which normal behaviour becomes abnormal behaviour. For example, at what point on the distribution curve does a person's IQ become abnormal?
- Some behaviour, such as depressive illness, is psychologically abnormal but not that rare.

Abnormality as behaviour which deviates from the social norm

Some people behave in socially deviant ways. Because their behaviour does not fit in with social norms or meet social expectations, they are seen as different. For example, a person who scavenges in dustbins and hoards rubbish in their home may be seen as abnormal. However, to suggest that behaving in a way that deviates from social norms defines abnormality has limitations:

- This definition could be used to discriminate against people of whom the majority disapprove and want to remove from society. For example, in the UK in the early part of the twentieth century, unmarried girls who became pregnant could be diagnosed as mentally ill and locked in asylums.
- Whether behaviour is seen as normal depends on its context. Preaching a sermon is seen as normal in a church, but preaching a sermon in a supermarket might be considered abnormal.
- Social norms and attitudes change. Homosexuality was believed to be a mental illness until the 1970s, but is not seen as such today.
- Social norms vary within and between cultures; there is not one universally acceptable set of social norms. In Muslim countries, a woman who dressed provocatively in public would be viewed as socially deviant, but this behaviour is common among women in Western society.

Abnormality as failure to function adequately

People who cannot look after themselves, or who are perceived to be irrational or out of control, are often viewed as abnormal. The problem with this is that it involves others in making value judgements about what it means to function adequately. The individuals themselves may not think they have a problem and their unusual behaviour may be a way of coping with their difficulties in life.

Abnormality as deviation from ideal mental health

Jahoda (1958) identified six conditions associated with ideal mental health:
1 a positive self-attitude and high self-esteem
2 a drive to realise self-potential (personal growth)
3 the ability to cope with stress
4 being in control and making your own decisions (personal autonomy)
5 an accurate perception of reality and the ability to feel for others
6 the ability to adapt to changes in one's environment

This approach also has limitations:
- The degree to which a person meets the six criteria may vary over time. Thus, the degree to which any individual can be defined as 'normal' might vary from day to day.
- It is a subjective standard — it is difficult to measure self-esteem and self-potential.
- It is an ethnocentric standard — it describes normality from an individualistic culture rather than from a collectivist one.
- By this standard, it is possible that most people could be defined as abnormal.

Cultural relativism in definitions of abnormality

A 'culture' is not a group of people, but the customs and attitudes that a group of people share. A 'sub-culture' is a group within a society that shares some practices with the dominant culture but which also has some special attitudes and customs.

Cultural relativism means that we cannot judge normality or abnormality without reference to the norms of the culture where the behaviour arose. Behaviour that may appear abnormal in one

Topic 1 Psychological abnormality

cultural setting, because it deviates from the norms of that culture, is not abnormal in its native cultural setting. Definitions of abnormality are limited because they are culturally specific.

A psychological abnormality can be said to be:
- **Absolute** — the disorder occurs with the same symptoms and with the same frequency in all cultures. This is probably true for schizophrenia.
- **Universal** — the disorder occurs in all cultures but not with the same frequency. This is true for some disorders, such as depression, which is more common, for example, in urban and industrial societies.
- **Culturally-relative** — the disorder is unique (or almost unique) to particular cultures and only meaningful within those cultures. These are called **culture-bound syndromes**.

Because cultures differ in their attitudes and customs, it is not possible to formulate absolute definitions of abnormality. For example, in the Trobriand Islands, it is normal for a son to clean the bones of his dead father and to give them to relatives to wear. It would be seen as abnormal for a widow not to wear the bones of her late husband. In the UK, this behaviour would be seen as abnormal (though in the Victorian age it was quite normal for a widow to wear rings and brooches woven from the hair of her deceased husband).

Item 2
Approaches to psychopathology

Biological approaches to psychopathology (abnormality) explore differences caused by genetics, biochemistry and brain anatomy. Psychological approaches to abnormality look at how early childhood experiences, family systems and the unconscious mind affect the way people behave, and how individuals differ in how they think about themselves and the world. Behaviourist approaches look at how the consequences of behaviour reinforce abnormal behaviour and thinking patterns. Each approach makes different assumptions about the causes of abnormality.

Item 3
The biological approach to psychopathology

The biological approach assumes that psychological abnormalities are symptoms of underlying physical causes. Thus, psychological disorders may be referred to as 'mental illnesses'. These are seen as arising from:
- **Genetics.** This is evidenced by the fact that some mental disorders, such as schizophrenia, run in families, suggesting an underlying genetic abnormality. Kety et al. (1994) found that in a sample of adoptees with chronic schizophrenia, the prevalence of the disorder was ten times higher in the biological relatives of the schizophrenic adoptees than in the biological relatives of the control group. This is evidence for the involvement of genetics in schizophrenia.
- **Infection.** Abnormalities may be caused by infection. General paresis is a condition involving mood swings and delusions and, eventually, paralysis and death. This is caused by syphilis and can now be treated with drugs.

- **Neurotransmitters.** These are biochemicals that carry the signals between brain cells. Too much or too little neurotransmitter may result in psychological disorders. For example, too much dopamine is thought to lead to schizophrenia.
- **Brain injury.** Patients who have suffered a stroke, particularly when the stroke damage is centred in the left hemisphere (in right-handed people), may lose their ability to understand and/or produce speech.

Evaluation of the biological approach

Strengths
- The approach does not blame people for their abnormal behaviour. It has led to a more humane treatment of the mentally ill.
- The scientific status and association with the medical profession means that this approach enjoys credibility.
- Objective evidence shows that biological causes can be linked to psychological symptoms, e.g. dopamine levels in schizophrenia.

Limitations
- Psychiatrists such as Szasz and Laing object to the medical approach. They see the use of labels, such as 'mentally ill', as a way of pathologising people whose behaviour we do not like or cannot explain.
- There may be problems of validity and reliability in diagnosing the type of abnormality. There is frequently a degree of overlap between symptoms of different disorders, meaning the diagnosis may be unreliable.
- The approach takes a reductionist approach to psychological abnormality and ignores the relationship between the mind and body.

Item 4
The behaviourist approach to psychopathology

The behaviourist approach makes three assumptions. First, it assumes that all behaviour is learned; second, that what has been learned can be unlearned; and third, that abnormal behaviour is learned in the same way as normal behaviour. This model sees the abnormal behaviour as the problem and not a symptom of an underlying cause.

Behaviourists propose that **classical conditioning** can explain phobias. In classical conditioning, an unconditioned stimulus, such as an unexpected loud noise, triggers a natural reflex, e.g. the startle response and fear. If another stimulus, such as seeing a spider, occurs at the same time, this may in future elicit the fear response. Watson and Rayner (1920) demonstrated how classical conditioning could explain the way in which fear could be learned.

Behaviourists also propose that abnormal behaviour can be learned by the process of **operant conditioning**, in which behaviour is learned through the consequences of our actions. If our actions result in rewarding consequences (positive reinforcement), or in something unpleasant ceasing (negative reinforcement), we will repeat the behaviour, but we will not repeat behaviour

Topic 1 Psychological abnormality

that has negative outcomes. Phobias such as fear of heights can be learned in this way. We become anxious at the thought of climbing the ladder, so we employ a window cleaner in order to avoid using a ladder, and this removes the anxiety (negative reinforcement).

Evaluation of the behaviourist approach

Strengths
- The approach proposes a simple testable explanation that is supported by experimental evidence.
- The behavioural approach is hopeful because it predicts that people can change (re-learn) their behaviour.

Limitations
- The approach is criticised as being dehumanising and mechanistic (Heather 1976). People are reduced to programmed stimulus–response units.
- The approach cannot explain all psychological disorders. Conditioning cannot cure all disorders, e.g. schizophrenia.

Item 5
The psychodynamic approach to psychopathology

The psychodynamic approach, based on Freudian theory, assumes that behaviour is motivated by unconscious forces, and that abnormal behaviour has its origins in unresolved, unconscious conflicts in early childhood. The model is based on Freud's proposal that the human personality comprises the id, the ego and the superego, and that the development of the personality progresses in five psychosexual stages (the oral, anal, phallic, latent and genital stages). According to the psychodynamic model, in childhood the ego is not fully developed, and is thus unable to manage the conflicting demands of the id and the superego. Conflict and anxiety may result and the ego defends itself by repression, projection or displacement. In repression, anxiety is hidden (repressed) into the unconscious, but stress in adulthood may trigger the repressed conflict, leading to psychological abnormality.

Evaluation of the psychodynamic approach

Strengths
- The approach identifies the importance of traumatic childhood experience in adult problems.
- Freud's theories changed people's attitudes to mental illness, and psychosomatic illnesses demonstrate the link between mind and body.
- The approach does not hold people responsible for their behaviour because the causes of behaviour are unconscious.

Limitations
- The approach is not scientific; Freud's theories are not falsifiable (his hypotheses are not testable).
- The approach overemphasises past experience, when clients' problems may have causes in the 'here and now'.
- The approach is reductionist and ignores biological and socio-cultural factors.

Item 6
The cognitive approach to psychopathology

The cognitive approach to abnormality is based on the assumption that the human mind is like an information processor and that people can control how they select, store and think about information. The cognitive approach proposes that to be normal is to be able to use cognitive processes to monitor and control our behaviour, and that abnormal behaviour is caused by faulty or irrational thoughts. In the cognitive approach, psychological problems are caused when people make incorrect inferences about themselves or others, and have negative thoughts about themselves and the future. **Beck and Clark (1988)** found that irrational beliefs were common in patients suffering anxiety and depression. For example, depressive people often believe that they are unloved, that they are failures as parents, and that nothing good will ever happen in the future.

Evaluation of the cognitive approach

Strengths
- The approach focuses on how the individual experiences the world and his or her feelings and beliefs, rather than relying on interpretations by other people.
- The approach is hopeful, as it assumes people have the power to change their behaviour.

Limitations
- The approach may encourage the idea that people are responsible for their own psychological problems, i.e. that they could be 'normal' if they so chose. This could lead to people being blamed for psychological abnormalities.
- The approach is reductionist as it ignores biological causes of psychological abnormality, such as genetics or biochemistry.

Item 7
Approaches to psychopathology: a comparison

Approach	Where problems originate	Criticism	Comment
Medical (biological) Abnormality is a symptom of underlying biological cause. Biology of brain/genes etc.	• Inside the person • May be inherited/genetic • Brain damage • Abnormal neuro-transmission	• Deterministic • Reductionist • No free will • Cannot explain why talking cures or conditioning are effective	• Ignores psychosocial factors but is scientific • Does not 'blame the individual' • Treatment = drugs/ECT

Topic 1 Psychological abnormality

Approach	Where problems originate	Criticism	Comment
Behaviourist Abnormal behaviour is learned and can be unlearned. Abnormal behaviour should be removed/treated.	• Abnormal behaviour is learned in interaction with the environment • Classical or operant conditioning/stimulus–response learning	• Deterministic/the past • No free will • Cannot explain why drugs or talking cures work	• Ignores biological factors • Does not 'blame the individual' • Treatment based on conditioning (learning)
Psychodynamic Unconscious conflict between ID — ego and superego. Behaviour is a symptom of an unseen cause.	• Inside the person • During early years e.g. Oedipus complex • Repression, regression • Ego defences	• Deterministic/the past • No free will • Unscientific, hard to collect empirical evidence • Cannot explain why drug treatment is effective	• Ignores biological factors • Does not blame the individual • Treatment = talking cure/psychoanalysis
Cognitive Mental processes not functioning properly.	• Inside the person • Irrational thoughts • Negative thinking, e.g. depression, 'awfulising'	• May 'blame' the individual — if you didn't think irrationally you wouldn't have a problem! • Cannot explain why drug treatment is effective	• Ignores biological and social factors • Treatment = talking cure/CBT

Item 8
Hypothetical case studies

1 Janus suffers from severe anxiety and has frequent panic attacks. He has been diagnosed as having an anxiety disorder.
2 Hector has been anxious and depressed since he became unemployed. He feels useless and knows he will never get another job.
3 Pandora has a severe snake phobia. She refuses to go on holiday with her family in case she sees a snake.

AQA (A) AS Psychology Unit 2 Section 3

Questions

1 Read your textbook and Item 1.

a Outline the main assumption of the statistical infrequency definition of abnormality.

b Describe the deviation from social norms definition of abnormality.

c How have psychologists defined ideal mental health?

d Explain *one* limitation of the statistical infrequency definition of abnormality.

e Explain *one* limitation of the deviation from social norms definition of abnormality.

f Suggest *one* reason why the definition of abnormality as a 'failure to function adequately' is not useful.

Topic 1 Psychological abnormality

2 Read your textbook and Item 1.

  a Explain what is meant by 'cultural relativism'.

  b Outline how psychologists could find out whether any psychological abnormality, such as depressive illness, is a universal phenomenon.

3 Read your textbook and Items 2 and 3.

  a Outline *two* assumptions of the biological approach to psychological abnormality.

  b Your friend is diagnosed as suffering from a depressive illness. Explain how a biological psychologist might explain his or her illness.

AQA (A) AS Psychology Unit 2 Section 3

c Describe *one* strength and *one* limitation of the biological approach to abnormality. Write two sentences and link them with the word 'however'.

4 Read your textbook and Item 4.

   a Outline *two* assumptions of the behaviourist approach to psychological abnormality.

   b Identify *two* processes that, according to the behaviourist model, may cause psychological abnormality.

   c Your friend is diagnosed as suffering from a depressive illness. Explain how a behaviourist psychologist might explain his or her illness.

   d Describe *one* strength and *one* limitation of the behaviourist model of abnormality.

Topic 1 Psychological abnormality

5 Read your textbook and Item 5.

a Outline *two* assumptions of the psychodynamic approach to psychological abnormality.

b Identify *two* factors that, according to the psychodynamic model, may cause psychological abnormality.

c Your friend is diagnosed as suffering from a depressive illness. Explain the assumptions made by a psychoanalyst when explaining his or her illness.

d Write a short paragraph outlining the strengths and limitations of the psychodynamic model of abnormality.

(Continued overleaf)

6 Read your textbook and Item 6.

a Outline *two* assumptions of the cognitive approach to psychological abnormality.

b Identify *two* factors that, according to the cognitive approach, may cause psychological abnormality.

c Your friend is diagnosed as suffering from a depressive illness. Describe how the cognitive approach to psychological abnormality explains depression.

d In two sentences, describe *one* strength and *one* limitation of the cognitive model of abnormality. Start the second sentence with the word 'however'.

Topic 1 Psychological abnormality

7 Read your textbook and Items 1–8. For *each* of the hypothetical cases in Item 8, describe the assumptions of either the biological model or any *one* psychological model of abnormality as to possible causes of the problem.

Assumptions of biological approach	Assumptions of psychological approach
Janus	Janus
Hector	Hector
Pandora	Pandora

8 Read your textbook and Items 1–7.

a You are the practice secretary and have been asked to take the minutes of the meeting at which Dr Gene (biological approach), Dr Freud (psychodynamic approach), Dr Sun (behaviourist approach) and Dr Cogito (cognitive approach) will discuss the case of Janus. Each doctor has put forward the key points of his/her explanation as to why Janus has developed an anxiety disorder. Outline what each doctor is likely to say.

	Why has Janus developed an anxiety disorder?
Dr Gene	
Dr Freud	
Dr Sun	
Dr Cogito	

b Complete the table to list *one* limitation for each of the doctors' explanations.

	Limitation of the explanation for Janus's anxiety disorder
Dr Gene	
Dr Freud	
Dr Sun	
Dr Cogito	

Topic 1 Psychological abnormality

9 *Exam practice*

Review your notes and Items 1–7. Discuss whether the biological model of abnormality can adequately explain psychological abnormality.

In your outline, identify the psychological evidence you will use and the evaluative points you will need.

Try to use one of these phrases for each evaluation point you list:
- One strength of this research is…
- On the other hand…
- This implies that…
- This is useful because…
- Not all psychologists agree, for example…
- There are advantages to X because…

Topic 2 Treating psychological abnormality

This topic focuses on treatments for psychological abnormality, including therapies based on the biological approach, such as drugs and ECT, and psychological therapies, including psychoanalysis, systematic desensitisation and cognitive behavioural therapy.

Item 1
Treatments based on the biological approach to abnormality

Treatments based on this approach assume that psychological abnormalities are symptoms of underlying physical causes.

- **Drug therapies (chemotherapy).** Anti-anxiety drugs, such as benzodiazepines, slow the activity of the central nervous system (CNS), reducing seratonin activity and anxiety and increasing relaxation. Beta-blockers act on the autonomic nervous system (ANS) to reduce activity in the ANS associated with anxiety — these drugs reduce heart rate, blood pressure and levels of cortisol. Anti-psychotic drugs can be used to reduce mental confusion and delusions. Anti-depressant drugs, such as Prozac, can be used to elevate mood. These treatments assume that an imbalance in biochemistry (neurotransmitters) is the cause of the abnormality.
- **Electroconvulsive therapy (ECT)** is a treatment in which a brief electrical stimulus is given to the brain via electrodes placed on the temples. The electrical charge lasts between 1 and 4 seconds, and causes an epileptic-like seizure. The amount of current needed to induce a seizure (the seizure threshold) can vary up to 40-fold between individuals. Most patients are given a total of 6–12 ECTs at a rate of one a day, three times a week. ECT is sometimes given to people with severe depression, which has not responded to other forms of treatment such as anti-depressants. It is usually only given after the risks have been explained and with the patient's consent. Side effects of ECT can include fear and anxiety, retrograde amnesia and headaches, and Rose et al. (2003) suggested that 33% of patients report long-term memory loss.

Evaluation of biological therapies

Advantages
- It is claimed that biological therapies (drugs) reduce the symptoms of conditions, such as schizophrenia, which formerly could not be treated.
- Drug therapy can be used alongside therapies based on psychological approaches.
- Drug treatments are easy to administer and do not involve the patient changing their lifestyle or behaviour.
- Drug therapies act rapidly to relieve symptoms.

Topic 2 Treating psychological abnormality

Limitations
- Biological therapies may cause ethical concerns. Some drug therapies can have unpleasant side effects. Patients with some conditions may be unable to understand the implications of their treatment and thus be unable to give their informed consent.
- Taking drugs may lead to addiction and dependency.
- Drugs may simply suppress the symptoms, not cure the disorder. The use of drugs may divert attention away from the real causes of the problem.
- Drug treatments take a reductionist approach to the treatment of abnormality because they ignore psychosocial factors.
- No one knows how or why ECT works, and it may cause serious side effects.

Item 2
Treatments based on the behaviourist approach to psychological abnormality

The treatments proposed by the behaviourist model are based on the assumption that abnormal behaviour is learned in the same way as normal behaviour and that it can be unlearned. Abnormal behaviour is seen as a 'problem to be cured'.

Behaviourists try to identify the **reinforcers** of abnormal behaviour and change the consequences of behaviour. Behavioural therapies may use:
- **classical conditioning** — in which an undesirable behaviour can be paired with an unpleasant response (aversion therapy)
- **systematic desensitisation** — in which phobics can be gradually reintroduced to a feared object or situation
- **token economies** — based on operant conditioning, which are often used in schools and hospitals to change the behaviour of delinquents and anorexics

Operant conditioning

Behavioural therapies based on operant conditioning assume that behaviour that brings about pleasurable consequences is likely to be repeated — such therapies are called **behaviour modification**. Behaviour modification can involve positive or negative reinforcement. In positive reinforcement, desired behaviour is rewarded by a pleasant consequence, because the use of a reward encourages the likelihood of the behaviour being repeated, e.g. if someone is praised for good work, this encourages (reinforces) its repetition. In negative reinforcement, desired behaviour is learned because the consequence of the behaviour is that 'something unpleasant' stops happening (or the patient escapes from an aversive stimulus), thus pleasure is felt. Behaviour modification usually involves schedules of reinforcement.

Behaviour modification programmes are used by clinical and educational psychologists to modify the behaviour of children or adults with challenging behaviour, and the ABC model is used to explain how behaviour modification programmes work:

A = the trigger (stimulus or event) that elicits the behaviour (the antecedent)
B = the behaviour
C = the consequences of the behaviour

Behaviour can be modified by changing either the antecedent or the consequence.

Applied behaviour analysis

Lovaas et al. (1967) first used operant conditioning in a technique called applied behaviour analysis (ABA) with autistic children who had little or no normal speech. A 'behaviour shaping' technique was used. First, verbal approval is paired with a piece of food (positive reinforcement) whenever the child makes eye contact or pays attention to the therapist's speech. The child is then reinforced with food or praise whenever any kind of speech sound is made. Once speech sounds occur without prompting, the therapist withholds rewards until the child successfully imitates/utters particular vowels or consonants, then words and finally combinations of words. Many reinforcements are needed before the child imitates simple phrases.

Systematic desensitisation

Systematic desensitisation is a type of behaviour therapy in which the undesired behaviour, for example a phobia, is broken down into the small stimulus–response units that comprise it.
It consists of:
- the construction of a hierarchy of fears
- training in relaxation — the relaxed state is incompatible with anxiety
- graded exposure (in imagination) and relaxation
- homework — practice in real life

For example, for a patient with a phobia of snakes, the least stressful situation might be to look at a picture of a snake, and the most stressful might be to touch a snake. The therapist works though each stimulus–response unit in the ascending hierarchy, helping the patient to replace each dysfunctional response of being afraid with the response of feeling relaxed. **McGrath et al. (1990)** report that 75% of phobic patients respond to systematic desensitisation. Following systematic desensitisation, 70% of patients show improvement in symptoms, but few patients are completely free of anxiety.

Token economy

A token economy is a behaviour modification technique used in psychiatric hospitals, prisons, schools etc. and involves the use of a reward (reinforcement) for desired behaviour that can be exchanged by the recipient for goods, services etc.

Neumark (1998) reports a token economy programme used at Wells Park, a residential school for children aged 7 to 11 with severe emotional or behavioural difficulties (EBD). The token economy system was introduced in 1990 and has been refined continually. Every 5 weeks, children, their families and teachers meet to decide and agree the children's 'targets'. Targets might be to 'keep still while I am talking', to 'use a quiet voice' or to 'write in smaller handwriting'. Every

Topic 2 Treating psychological abnormality

15 minutes from Monday to Friday, each child has an opportunity to receive a token, and every day at 3.45 the children can 'cash in' tokens in groups of five called 'giants' for treats such as books, toys or extra play. More ambitious children can save up 'giants' for shopping trips or outings. The token economy is effective because all the teachers operate the system in the same way, and children described previously as unteachable or hyperactive sit down and read and enjoy learning and can increase their reading age by 2 or 3 years in the first year at the school.

Evaluation of behaviourist therapies

Strengths
- Behaviourist therapies are effective for treating phobias, obsessive–compulsive disorders and eating disorders, and are appropriate for those whose symptoms are behavioural.
- The behavioural model is hopeful because it predicts that people can change (re-learn) their behaviour.

Limitations
- Token economies involving reinforcers that withhold a basic human right, such as food, clothing or privacy, are unethical. These procedures have been ruled illegal in the USA.
- These therapies are only effective for a limited number of disorders — conditioning cannot cure all disorders, e.g. schizophrenia.

Item 3
Treatments based on the psychodynamic approach to psychological abnormality

These treatments are based on the assumption that abnormal behaviour is motivated by unconscious forces, and are focused on three objectives: first, to free healthy impulses; second, to strengthen and re-educate the ego; and third, to change the superego so that it causes less anxiety. This is achieved by psychoanalysis, during which dream analysis and free association may be used. In free association, based on the idea that the ego will try to repress unacceptable impulses, the therapist interprets pauses or hesitations when talking about certain topics as signs of repressed anxiety. In dream analysis, based on Freud's proposal that dreams represent unconscious wish-fulfilment, the therapist interprets dreams as symbols of repressed wishes. By using thematic apperception tests, the client may reveal unconscious thoughts which the therapist interprets. In the process of transference, the client transfers repressed conflicts onto the therapist, who 'becomes the parent' the child lacked or needed to resolve the unconscious conflict.

Evaluation of psychodynamic therapies

Strengths
- Freud's theories changed people's attitudes to mental illness, and psychotherapy has been found to be effective in psychosomatic illnesses.

Limitations
- Eysenck (1952) found that 66% of patients in therapy recover within 2 years, but so do 66% of patients who have no therapy.
- Psychoanalysis may only benefit certain clients — the young, attractive, verbal, intelligent and successful (the YAVIS model) — and are more likely to be effective with clients who have a positive attitude (belief) towards therapy (a self-fulfilling prophesy).
- The treatment takes a long time and is expensive.

Item 4
Treatments based on the cognitive approach to psychological abnormality

Treatments based on this approach focus on helping the patient change irrational or negative thoughts to ones that are rational and positive. The objective of treatment is to correct unrealistic ideas, by mean of cognitive restructuring, so that thinking becomes an effective means of controlling behaviour. The therapist supports the patient through a process of cognitive behaviour therapy (CBT) until thought processes become more rational. Examples of treatments based on the cognitive model are rational emotive therapy for depression (Beck 1976) and stress inoculation training (Meichenbaum).

Rational emotive behaviour therapy (REBT)

Ellis (1975) developed rational emotive therapy, based on the idea that some people have persistent self-defeating thoughts that are irrational. According to Ellis, irrational beliefs that may cause needless upset can be identified when we catch ourselves thinking 'should' or 'must' in ways that are subjective and judgemental. Thoughts such as 'I **must** be approved of by everybody' or 'I **should** always achieve in everything I do' are irrational and believing these, or similar, irrational statements is self-defeating, because this way of thinking prevents us from taking constructive action to change ourselves, or to change the situation. REBT aims to challenge this way of thinking by helping clients to recognise their irrationality and the consequences of their habitual way of thinking. Clients are taught to recognise and replace their 'irrational' thoughts with more constructive and realistic ones. As with behaviour modification, an ABC model can be used to explain what happens in REBT:

A We experience an **activating event**, leading to emotional arousal (e.g. receiving a poor grade in an exam).

B A **belief** is developed about the event that may be rational (e.g. 'I would have done better if I had revised more effectively') or irrational (e.g. 'I must be thick and don't deserve to do better').

C Behavioural **consequences** ensue from our beliefs, which may be productive (e.g. deciding to re-sit the exam and revising hard) or unproductive (e.g. dropping out of class).

Topic 2 Treating psychological abnormality

In REBT, a person is encouraged to realise that it is not the 'events in themselves' that lead to negative consequences, but the self-defeating beliefs that we develop about the events. Clients are encouraged to change the way they think about events in their lives by:
- **logical disputing** — asking themselves whether the way they think 'makes sense'
- **empirical disputing** — asking themselves whether there is proof that their belief is accurate
- **pragmatic disputing** — asking themselves whether the way they think is helpful to them

Effective internal disputation changes self-defeating beliefs into more rational ones that help the client feel better about him/herself.

Evaluation of the cognitive therapies

Strengths
- Therapy focuses on how the individual experiences the world and his/her feelings and beliefs, rather than relying on interpretations by other people.
- Cognitive-based therapies may increase self-efficacy and self-belief, and thus improve people's lives.
- Supporting evidence from Hollon et al. (1992) found CBT was more effective than drugs for treating depression and anxiety.

Limitations
- Treatments may only be effective for people who have good problem-solving skills, an insight into their behaviour and the willingness to spend time on 'the problem'.
- Treatments may only be effective for anxiety disorders and depressive illnesses. They may not be generalisable to many psychological abnormalities.

Questions

1 Read your textbook and Item 1.

   a Your friend is diagnosed as suffering from a depressive illness. Suggest how a biological psychologist might treat a depressive disorder.

b Describe *one* strength and *one* limitation of the use of drugs in the treatment of psychological abnormalities. Write two sentences and link them with the phrase 'on the other hand'.

2 Read your textbook and Item 2.

a Your friend is diagnosed as suffering from a depressive illness. Suggest how a behaviourist psychologist might treat a depressive disorder.

b Describe *one* strength and *one* limitation of the use of behaviour therapies to treat psychological abnormalities. Write two sentences and link them with the phrase 'on the other hand'.

3 Read your textbook and Item 3.

a Your friend is diagnosed as suffering from a depressive illness. Describe *one* method of treatment that is associated with the psychodynamic model.

Topic 2 Treating psychological abnormality

b You are a well-known psychoanalyst and you have been asked to write a magazine article describing 'the characteristics of people who will benefit from psychoanalysis'. From what you have learned about the psychodynamic model of abnormality, describe the 'ideal patient'. (**Hint:** describe the *characteristics* of the patient.)

4 Read your textbook and Item 4.

   a Your friend is diagnosed as suffering from a depressive illness. Describe *one* method of treatment that is associated with the cognitive approach.

   b In two sentences, describe *one* strength and *one* limitation of using cognitive restructuring therapies to treat psychological abnormalities. Start the second sentence with the words 'on the other hand'.

5 Read your textbook and Items 1–4.

Petronella has a phobia of spiders (arachnophobia). Even thinking that there may be a spider somewhere causes her great anxiety and she is afraid to go outside in case there is a spider anywhere. In an attempt to overcome her phobia, she consults a behaviourist psychologist.

Explain how systematic de-sensitisation might be used to overcome Petronella's phobia of spiders.

Topic 2 Treating psychological abnormality

6 Read Items 1–4.

For more than a month, Rosie has been feeling very anxious and stressed. Discuss the extent to which cognitive behavioural therapy may be an effective way to treat stress.

7 Exam practice

All biological treatments change how the brain and/or body works, and all treatments have side effects.

Drug treatment has been shown to be an effective treatment for some mental disorders and may allow people to live 'almost normal' lives, but all drugs have side effects that may vary from person to person.

To what extent is drug treatment an effective and appropriate way to treat mental disorders?